For Those Who Cry Wolf

by: Mecko Gibson

For Those Who Cry Wolf

© 2017 Mecko Gibson
All rights reserved

First Edition
Mecko Gibson
ISBN-13: 978-0-9995456-0-7
ISBN-10: 0999545604

Cover Art By: Mecko Gibson
Edited By: Nikera Cartwright
Published By: Mecko Gibson

Social Media: Twitter - Meck0
                 Instagram - MeckoGibsonArt

For Family, Friends and Strangers...

Sometimes we find friends in the three;
other times we find strangers in the two.

Let's hope for the former.

Acknowledgments

On the first draft of this very page, I had a list of about 65 names tightly bunched together. My then-editor, Mike (yeah, let's call him Mike), queried as to why would I take up so much time and space with so many names. He didn't like my reasoning much, and, I suppose, I shouldn't have expected him to, for few would ever understand how much every *'like', 'retweet', or 'comment'* helps during the creative process.

I know, regardless of how many drafts I type, or how many pages I allot, I won't be able to thank you all, and for that I am truly sorry. So instead of making a list of names to thank, I'll simply make a statement:

To anyone that was (or still is) a classmate, friend, family or associate of mine, I thank you. Your critiques and support, whether solicited or not, were more than I could ever ask for and I'm sorry that I can't give you all the individual acknowledgments that you truly deserve. Please accept my thanks and know that, if I had more, it would all be yours.

- Mecko

Prelude –
For Those Who Cry Wolf I

Dear you,

Scream if you can
Whisper if you can't
And know that
If you never speak another word
We'll hear you

Our hearts are fluent in silence

For we, too, are wolves
And our pact is just as strong.

- *Arh-woooouuu.*

Part I: Her

– Stories of affections, rejections
and survival; mostly, survival.

Based On
A True Story...

Stories I

She once told me a story
about a wave
that left her lonely
only to come crashing home
without warning…

Intent on getting her wet;
sometimes gentle
sometimes rough

Princess of a castle
built of sand
and not of rock

Some nights he knocks,
some nights she weeps

Because late at night
when the world's asleep
his heart isn't the only thing that beats.

—Splash.

Beauty I

Today…I met *Beauty*.

And though the beast in me was properly chained,
I fell victim to her smile;
my weakest link.

The next few hours were *beautiful*.

Intoxicated by conversation
my eyes went drunk driving;
I sped past my present's future
and rode a daydream into forever.

I couldn't stop.
I *wouldn't* stop;
for all I saw was green…in her eyes.

In her eyes is where my entire life changed.

I was a fire;
feral, obstinate and swift.
But like a flame caught by a wick,
my passion conceived prudence,
and like wax kissed by a flame,
all doubt that there was a one—
that she was the one
                melted
                    away.

Beauty II

Yesterday...I met *Beauty.*

Beauty stood at about five foot five
with two brown eyes that coloured
inside lines I swore I'd never cross again.

She was my sky.
And like a kite without a tail,
recklessly, my emotions flew;
a one way ticket to cloud nine.

The rest of the day was *beautiful...*

In between heaven and earth
we played a game of forever;
gambling our non-fiction like savings
on fiction-like dreams.

We bungee-jumped from stars
and surfed rainbows into eternal sunsets.
Stopping only to read Cupid's copy of
"*Loving Her for Dummies.*"

And since love and life couldn't seem to play nice,
I often wish heaven made two
because my heart and my soul found it hard to share you.

For indeed,
you must be some rare kind of extraordinary
if even in my dreams I day-dream of you.

Beauty III

Once upon a time...I met *Beauty*.

And though briefly we touched,
strangely,
like a scar,
she left a mark.

I now understand why
forty-four days into a new year
people go crazy;
I, myself, have gone crazy...
walking miles on knees
reciting *"don't leave,"*
in every language,
"Please..."

I apologized for sins never committed
in hopes that she could see that I was committed...
committed to carrying her cross
instead of being a cross
on her "to-do" list.

I never thought she'd do it;
leave,
sans reason.

In the middle of a future built for two,
she chose one.

But never-the-less in every loneliness I play a sunrise,
strumming sunsets on a six-stringed butterfly
that longed for the days it shared a cocoon.

And though it was a far drive away
other heartbroken stars came to play.

On that day
my fingers brought every string to life,
wondering if she ever knew
that—
for her,
        I bled myself dry.

Beauty IV

A lot has changed since I first met *Beauty.*

I went from a lover of lions to a photographer of
    butterflies;
    singing "Three Little Birds..." at the smile of
    morning's window.

Since her I've contradicted my every diction...
confusing fiction and non-fiction
with a new found addiction of scripting my own
    endings.

Since her I've sky-dived from Pluto
and painted portraits on Mars.

Since her I've lived a mirage
and dined in its oasis.

Since her I've sailed sinking ships through dry deserts
in search of the treasure we buried
for the future she now carries...
for someone else.

Since her I've broken hearts in search of parts
that could rebuild what we once had.

Since her I've died; twice.
Thrice resurrected with the same heart that was
    sentenced to death
    for not choosing life–without *her.*

Without her–
I'm a form of my former self.

Without her,
I'm just a puppet;
a mortal marionette manipulated by loss,
reminiscing in the romantic irony that *Beauty* was
    my strings.

Lessons

He taught me how to–
tie ties.

But *never* told me that one could be used to choke a
woman.

She's still breathing.
I know.
She's strong that way.

Strong in a way I wish I was...

Because if I was...
I'd–

Use the same pan that he said was perfect for pancakes
to hit him harder than he hit her...
instead of being hit harder
than
    he
      hit
        her.

At ten years old he taught me how
to take a punch like a man.

I just wish, then, that I knew
how to hit like one, too.

To Whom It May Concern:

Dear,

Ms. Unknown,
Ms. Broken Home,
Ms. Broken Heart,
Ms. All Alone,

Ms. Lonely Lips,
Ms. Can't Do This Shit,
Ms. Torn Apart,
Ms. Just For The Kids,

Ms. I Wear The Pants,
Ms. One More Chance,
Ms. I Gave My All,
Ms. One Last Stand,

Ms. 9-5,
Ms. 5-9.
Ms. Always On Call,
Ms. He's Never on Time,

Ms. Victim of Lies,
Ms. Teary Eyes,
Ms. Work Never Done,
Ms. Woman No Cry,

Ms. Sleepless Nights,
Ms. Too Many Fights,
Ms. Nowhere To Run,

Ms. Tina And Ike,

Ms. Life's Too Hard,
Ms. Till Death Do Us Part,
Ms. I've Had Enough,
Ms. It Died From The Start,

Ms. Just Can't Quit,
Ms. Bobby and Whit,
Ms. Lost In Lust,
Ms. Back In It,

Ms. No Respect,
Ms. I'll Never Let…,
Ms. On the Low,
Ms. Just for Sex,

Ms. Maybe He'll Change,
Ms. We're Too Much The Same,
Ms. Poppy Show,
Ms. He Called the Wrong Name,

Ms. Believing His Lies,
Ms. Chick On The Side,
Ms. He Took It By Force,
Ms. I'm Leaving This Time,

Ms. For Years I Served,
Ms. I Got What I Deserved,
Ms. I Need A Divorce,
Ms. On My Last Nerve,

Ms. Damnit I've Tried,
Ms. Not Satisfied,
Ms. Murder She Wrote,
Ms. Suicide,

Ms. No More Wife,
Ms. No More Life,
Ms. Murder She Spoke,
Ms. Ended Her Life...

And to all the others,
I just wanted you to know:

You're stronger than Samson ever was
and fought battles no man could.

To men, you fell short
but, still, tall you stood.

Through your tears you brought boy
and through your love that boy became man,
for that I am thankful,

Yours truly,
                    Mr. I understand.

Of Monsters and Men

Sometimes the men she loves become monsters.
Sometimes the monsters she loves become men.

(un)Planned Parenthood

At two weeks old,
He was two weeks sold,
Into death by the breath
Of two weak souls.

(un)Planned Parenthood II

That which should've brought us together has torn us apart.

Together we were to forever–*laugh*...
as we planned a future where you would never cry.

But since that final time you did
our plans went to shit,
and it's only a matter of time
before 'ours' becomes 'mine'

Half of hers
lost in words
I can no longer find.
                              –R.I.P.

Diary I

I never owned a diary...
but if I did
it would be filled with crayon-written confessions
and etch-o-sketched dreams.

Scribbled on the screen would be the pathetic
penmanship of an adult that still plays *Pokémon*
hoping to one day evolve into your favourite
colour.

Diary II

I never owned a diary...
but if I did
it would secure my silliest soliloquies
and my insane plan to build a Lego bridge that'll lead
me to wherever you are...
because—
whoever you are
has stolen my attention
and has given me new reasons
to breathe.

Kisses I

Her kiss was like a Hurricane...
And I, a lonely palm,
could do nothing but sway
as she tip-toed to catch me
before I blew away...

It was during this exchange
that I tried to define
the thin line between
natural disaster and phenomenon.

Kisses II

Her kiss was like a handshake...
firm– at first,
but ever so soft as we released.

Synergies synchronized in ways that secured encores
for an audience of two,
with space in between for
none.

#MeToo

She, too,
Said "me too",
When he–
Too familiar with fingers
Forced four
Between hers
Each eager
To teach her–
'A *special* kind of love.'

She, too–

          "Trusting,"
                "Lusting,"
                        "Fast,"
                            and
                                  "Friendly"

is what those called *family* say...
To explain the day
their preteen
was raped…

By the same cousin
that doesn't understand
that the phrase,

"If we weren't cousins..."

Is a creepy thing to say...

But that was way way back then,
When they were 9 or 10,
Just *young* kids,
Saying dumb shit,
This, this, this is different...

It's *her fault* she—
kissed him...
On the cheek when he asked,
She *should've known better* than to wear those short pants
Whenever he came around...

Because he's not safe to be around...

And that's no family secret,
So to hold her accountable for
Not being powerful
Enough
To stop his lust...
                    is fucked up.

The same cousin or uncle
You don't trust around your purse...
You trust
Around her...

She, too,
said "me too"
When he too,
Took her two legs,
and said,

"No one has to know."

But now everyone knows
And no...
It's not her fault
She lost a fight
That—
You once fought,
But now she's caught,
Lost in between
Secrets families keep safe
To avoid public shame...

She, too,
said

> "Me too, I was to blame,
> For 'lying' about him trying
> To do certain things,
> And no it's not fair,
> To fear shame,
> It's fucked up
> That such love
> Shares last names…"

She, too,
Said "me too",
As groups who,
Came to
Heal,
Held hands
Cos they, too,
Felt hands
And…
As a man

I stood or stand
With them
Cos
I, too,
Was a 'me too'
That kept truths
From those who
Knew who
Touched who
Back then
So when
They spoke
I choked
Cause I know,
How they– ...
Wow they– ... ...
"Sister may I–I'm so sorry,
I–I–..."
Stopped mid sentence.

Because she who,
Planted a garden of 'me toos'
Rose...

Like Mewtwo,
She who,
Was once too weak to
Stab or seek help,
Stood strong,
Spoke up
and said,
                    Nothing.

Consent

She said *no,*
in a language that
few men understood

(mis)Taking her insistence
for permitted persistence
as if rejection was just another invitation
to *try*
     again.

Kings

Her body was a temple
broken and defiled
by the same men
that crowned her queen
but denied her throne.

Music

We made music before we made love;
slow dancing to heartbeats
that struggled to sync.

Skin to skin conversations
percussed without hesitation

For we were a song
long before we were ever
"patient"
or
"kind."

And I'm inclined
to believe that—
the lyrics composed in sex, sweat and sheets
were far better than the ones we composed
in love.

Swim Good

She doesn't know how to swim
and I don't know how to love...

So feet first we fall,
head over heels
into rivers that lust more than run.

We're drowning
again
and it's a pity
we never learned how
to swim.

First

She was his first.

And for the second time
they became one.

Second

He called her fat.

And for the first time
since their first time
she came
second.

Without Me

Without me she soared.
Spreading her wings between pages
I've long turned.

She's a run on sentence that my presence has slowed
since me we all agree that even higher she's flown.

I was never her inspiration
Period.

Never her next paragraph in a sentence
that's two weeks late.

Never the Samson that removed those blocks
from her paper.
I was just a boy she met on her quest from now to later.

And while it's strange that we're strangers,
I'm happy to hear that she's happy again.
Spreading her wings between the pages we bent.

She's written a lifetime since that day that we said
"Forever..." and meant it.
I still do.

I just wish I could write her away, too.

Bridges

We crossed bridges we should've burned
And burned bridges we should've crossed

Ad Lib

"Just be yourself," they said.
As if they forgot that my words
never remember their lines;
rehearsed scripts playing tug-of-war with lips that
ad-lib
every time
they
see
you.

Muse

She's
an immortal goddess
with nine lives
that die
every time
he decides...
to leave.

Muse II

She's a paint brush without a parachute—
diving excuse first
into dried up colours
that refuse to bleed
for her...

Muse III

She's a work of art;
a Rembrandt that left remnants of rhyme
in her every reason
as to why
she and I
would never be
more than
friends.

Muse IV

I was wrong to suggest
that our friendship meant she owed
me a date I never asked for;

Wrong to suggest that I was overlooked
for a chance that she never denied.

I Wonder

I wonder if she knows...
that despite the fact he doesn't have my nose,
I'd still give;

I'd still give my left lung if he needed one;
sacrificing half a breath
just so that he can hold his.

I wonder...

I wonder if she knows
that even though our ears are different
to him I'd still listen;

Saving an eardrum for his every heartbeat
because it doesn't take identical blood types
for two hearts to play in rhythm.

I wonder...

I wonder if she knows
that even though we don't share DNA
I'd never go M.I.A...

In fact,
the age difference in between us would be as far as I
would ever be distant...

As my brain learns how to teach him
and my heart learns how to miss him.

I wonder...

I wonder if she knows...
that even though he belongs to another
I'd still treat him as my own.

Because although I am guarded
for him I have added
a second room in this heart called
home.

Covers

I judged a book by her cover
and as a result
I never made it past the contents.

Queen

I'm in love with a goddess that demeans her being
by simply being content
with the contents
of being
      queen.

The Buffet

I met her at the buffet.
She was starving for attention
but duly mentioned she had enough on her plate.

And judging by the size of her eyes
I guess I'd have to agree.
A steady diet of domestic violence
made it hard for her to see...

a future.

Her soups were seasoned with tasted tears
and washed away with bloody water.
She no longer had a taste for whine
because every time she did
he'd hit her high pitch with a swing
in places that made it hard to swallow

her past.

She once asked if
I ever tasted my last breath.
A bitter recipe that involved two hands and one neck
best served over screams for help.

An acquired taste I'm sure
as she implored that the recipe was a family secret that
she first received

as a present.

A wedding gift perfectly wrapped with slaps that gave
birth to frozen fears,
defrosted by the aborted promises that
                    he'll
                    never
                    do
                        it
                        again...

But he did.

Half cooked lies for dinner
as he fed her fist after fist.

Which probably explains the bruises that I once
thought were stains
of *beauty*.

They were love bites I assumed as she consumed the
one thing that was truly delectable;
her heart.

See for years she had prepared it to be one day served
    to a knight;
    her body a table dressed in white and her eyes the
    candlelight...
    he would enjoy how they flickered.

But instead of serving him,
he served her...
rum punches that distorted her figure.

She hated when he drank
for she was allergic to kisses that taste like liquor.

Kisses that evolved into fists that would eventually lick
her...*over and over again.*

She then–
had the heart to ask if I was ok.
But the irony of such a question gave me an
indigestion that took my appetite away.

I no longer hungered for her youth.
In that moment, I sought atonement;
I no longer craved her forbidden fruit.

She fed me a taste of the years she faced
and I felt like I bit of more than I could chew.

I spilled her glass of emotions
without the notion of what she'd probably been
through.

On the table were restraining orders, fermented tears
and a history of abuse.

Strange food indeed.
I contemplated vacating
but such a table I couldn't leave.

Because I still saw the beauty her past tried to hide.
I wasn't much of a waiter
but I was prepared to serve her mind,
though lost in her past was a heart she may never find.

I'm not much of a waiter
but there's patience in this heart of mine.
So when she asks what's for dinner
I simply answer
                "mine."

Flames

Once upon a time there was a smile,
Erased by a flame;
A flame that never burned brighter than mine
But still lit her heart on fire
Though, not surprisingly,
Shortly thereafter,
Going out
With the wind.

Choices

I guess I'll have to choose this time,
between war of heart and peace of mind.
Because ever since you gave *him* piece of mine,
I lost hope but found time.

Time to take big steps on thin ropes
knowing it's a long way to recovery
and a long way down if I ever fall for your claims of
    you still loving me.

Are you still loving me?

Because, I mean, God said to forgive
and for you I'd give what's left of me;
those parts that studied even though you cheat.

And if you ever again can love *just me,*
or somehow find enough to love both of us...
you know where to find me;

Hiding under the biggest rock,
near the bottom,
scavenging for another you.

Teacher

They say you live and you learn
but I don't understand Love's class

If you try hard, you fail,
But yet the cheaters seem to pass?

Teacher?
I hate to ask
but you see, I was never really *good* at math…

So is it because I put her first,
the reason why it never lasts?

See,
between me, her and *math,*
we have an emotional triangle.
She's looking for x
and I'm looking for that complementary angle.
But see where we don't agree,
is at the three hundred and sixtieth degree
so now she's my x and I'm wondering y
we never made it to z.

Now I'm–
ready to cheat…
and ask lust for a few favours.
Trade her three kisses
and a chick-o-stick,
for the answers to now and later.

Then maybe *now,*
or *later,*
This problem I'd understand…
See the only problem I have with falling in love
is finding a way to stay down.

So Gravity, won't you help me please
I'm trying to fall where the grass is green.
Where cards and chess cease to exist,
because I need a queen that doesn't play games.

So Teacher won't you help me please
if only just this once.
I've subtracted the asses,
divided second chances,
but still can't find the one…

So Teacher, won't you help me please,
this problem I need to solve,
because I'm about to go from trying too hard
to no longer trying at all.

Pictures

They say a picture is worth a thousand words
so it's funny how I never knew
that there were over a thousand words
without the letter 'U'.

Humans

Out of the many,
I've found but two,
And lost them both,
When I lost you.

My Heroin, My Heroine

I've been picking flowers for hours,
my thoughts won't seem to stop
playing this game with your name;

"She loves me, she loves me not."

And for each *'she loves me'*,
my world seems to spin,
I'm addicted to your thoughts,
your voice is like heroin.
You are my heroine,
please rescue me;
imprisoned by Hope,
for fighting Gravity.

And while I slept,
you smiled at me.
Our kisses played "Catch"
in my every dream.

And in between in-betweens,
my pain slaves for you,
so you can have your cake
and eat it too.

I'm falling for you
come rescue me.
I got high off your thoughts,
pushed by Gravity.

Please free-fall with me
through window-panes.
My thoughts sleep naked,
but you dress my dreams.

I'm falling for you
and it's not impossible to see
that if God made you
he must really love me.

I'm falling for you,
blame Gravity,
my heroin, my heroine,
please rescue me.

Breakup

She left him like 4:57 on a Friday afternoon.

Reciprocity

Love has a habit of leaving
before I'm ready to reciprocate.

Because of Me

Your hate, my love,
is much to bear,
and thus lies the irony;

Your pain, my love,
is my own fault,
we hurt because of me.

For You…

I'll paint a song
that sings cross the page
or draw a flavour
that sweetens with age.
I'll speak a rose
that never dies
or write a tear
that never cries.
I'll listen to a touch
that speaks its heart
or taste a dream
of beauty and art.
I'll water a flame
'till it grows
or watch eyes of blind
and secrets they show.
I'll marry a face
that smiles with time
or colour a future
of rhythm and rhyme.
For you I'm different
in winters I'll shine,
I'll do the impossible
to make you mine.

She Said

She said,

I want you to fuck me while you're still charming.
Let's combust before your wick lets go
like everyone else.

She Said II

She said,

You know my body better than I do.
But don't think that you know me.
Just because you fuck me doesn't mean that you
know me.

She Said III

She said,

You smell like passion and vulnerability.
Take me, before you realize your worth.

She Said IV

She said,

If I cut out my tongue would your love still taste the
same?

She Said V:
A Broken Record

She said,
I'm…broken
So please don't try to fix me.
My spirits are down
but please don't try to lift me…
because I'm a few pounds overweight…

But I'm not fat.

It's just that—
my heart…is heavy.
And the bags my eyes carry aren't as light as they use
to be.
They grew bigger with each nigga that felt the need
to put a bruise on me.

I bruise easily.

But maybe…it's my fault.
My fault because greedily I ate up the sweet lies that
men fed to me.
Considered ungrateful because a taste full of cuffed
knuckles weren't enough for me.
I was fully clothed with faith
but they plucked all my trust from me.
Left me naked with this hatred
for any man that looked at me lustfully.

They made me believe that perhaps it sucks to be
        lovely...
Judge me,
but honestly,
sometimes I wish I was ugly
so they would think twice before they hug me.
It bugs me,
To men, life is Jumanji;
they pursue you like gentlemen but choose to love you
        like monkeys.
I'm clumsy,
always falling for dumb shit.
I'm stuck in an endless cycle,
they treat me like laundry;
they continue to wear me out...

I– have many doubts...
I'm so confused…
Is this what love is supposed to feel like?
A yo-yo?
They throw me down and pick me up whenever they
        feel like?

I just wish…to feel liked.
I just wish…to feel loved.
I just wish to be…missed.

I wish someone would just miss me,
instead of hit me.
I'm a sweet girl, but please, please don't lick me.
As tempting as it may be…

Judge me,
but honestly,
sometimes I wish I weighed 300 hundred pounds.
I wish I were heavy,
so they wouldn't shove me around.
They just push and push and push
but yet wonder why I'm so distant.

I'm so distant that I just wish someone would get in
    touch with me
instead of touch me.
Love me
instead of fuck me.
Call me baby instead of giving me babies to raise on
    my own.

I was once a family
but now I reside in a reality where the best parts of
    me are long gone.

See I lost my heart about three relationships ago,
and ever since my trust caught me in between the
    sheets of another lie, it packed its backs and vowed
    never to return.
And now you stand here telling me that you wish to
    earn... my trust?
My heart?
You stand here telling me that you wish to–fix me?
Heh, well, baby...
I'm...broken
(continue from line 3)

Liar, Liar I: Puppets

She thinks men are all puppets with noses that
surpass the length of their strings.

Liar, Liar II: Cannibals

She ate up his lies
but fed him the same.

Crash

You have my love
I feel your pain
Into my genes
You've stitched your name
You've fixed my ears
They inhale your moans
In my lungs
Your kisses
Found home
From Venus to Mars
My arms you ride
I don't know the way
But I follow your eyes
To infinity and beyond
My legs
Your throne
As two hips form
New Chromosomes
Lost in the moment
Swimming in sound
Floating in tears
In your sheets we drown
And for the moment
I taste the sweetest sin
Your pleasures measured
By the scars in my skin
I breathe your presence
Your heart beats my past
And through your Eve
Our Adam will pass
See time plays tricks
From memories I'm torn
As I crash into reality
His smile is born.

Again

If Heaven has an artist,
Then yesterday was her masterpiece,
She painted of you, a beautiful view,
That stole my will to speak.

Though stolen, my moment
(to say much more),
I'll never forget how it felt,
To stand and smile, while all the while,
Falling for you,
Again.

EBGDAE

Oh please, oh please let her sing today,
her strings they bring such a feel my way.

Frozen I am, a slave to her sounds,
I get high off her verbs, seduced by her nouns.

Whenever she plays, my hearts seems to pause,
she's killing me softly, I hang by her chords.

She's singing my thoughts, she's reading my mind,
kidnapped by her strums held hostage in rhyme.

This must be a crime,
Officer please...
her voice is a weapon; a threat when she sings.

Officer, officer,
arrest her please,
my heart has been stolen by her six strings.

I'd like to press charges,
I know each one by name...
They hide in disguise as
E, B, G, D, A, E.

My Favourite Soliloquy

I'm falling for a distant memory
So clumsy when I start remembering
The way her smile held hands
With all of God's plans

Her smile;
My favourite soliloquy.

Lost Ones

About three errors ago I met perfection.
Flawless in her frown she smiled at a world that
    worshipped her existence.
I remembered how she would lend her beauty to the
    beaches,
mentoring the orphaned waves as they swam on by.

Time after time I tried to swim alongside her,
but for some reason I never made it past the shore;
shallow thoughts restrained me from going too deep;
from drowning myself in endless possibilities.

Intimidated by her genetic make-up
I concealed the foundation set by Destiny.
Creating a destination where expectations never expect
    to be.

Truthfully, I admire her beaut,
Lost in Eden heaven has hidden its sweetest fruit.

Sweet, but hard to reach,
and easily bruised.
So to avoid a fourth error I made a fourth error;
I never pursued.

I never chased the perfect catch
and now I'm caught by thoughts that won't let me go.
A prisoner to the whisperer that shouts

    "let her know…"

One day I will, one day I may,
confess the mess that my heart has made.
One day I will, one day I may,
chase the one that got away.

Premature

"I love you too,"
she said,
prematurely.

After awaiting an "I love you"
that never came.

Her...

Lost in *His* arms,
I found her;
the lady I was purposed to seek.

But in the middle of her praise,
like Adam I hid afraid,
in God's presence I dared not speak.

For who am I to desire,
the beauty angels admire,
if my praises are still slaves to sin?

So until they're set free,
to her I'll just be,
someone her father won't ever let in.

But like Jacob, I'd take up 14 years of service,
I'd labour and commit my all,
and though I still may lose her, I won't be a loser,
in His service I can suffer no loss.

One day, I may, say more than hello,
but I promise I won't dare say more,
until my heart acquiescently quits this world,
and starts working full-time for God.

*–I think one of the noblest things a guy can do for a girl is to leave
her alone until he's absolutely positive he wants to commit...It's not
fair for you to waste her time while you're trying to figure out how
to use yours. Don't walk her across a bridge you haven't built yet...*

Her III

—At some point in your life you do what you have to,
to get the girl that you have to have;
And I just have to have Her...

I'm trying to deserve her,
but there are greater men than me,
like a Samson or Jacob, a Daniel or David;
a King to better serve a Queen.

I'm trying to deserve her,
but my sins are stronger than me,
I'm failing as a disciple,
I envy and idle,
I anger, I lust, I greed.

I'm trying to deserve her,
but I'm not the hero she seeks,
imprisoned amongst the living,
her beauty God has hidden,
in a place my faith can't reach.

I'm trying to deserve her,
so while other men tend to their thirst,
I'm starving for her father to shelter me with armour
until my last name is strong enough to carry her first.

Her IV

I wonder if she'll forgive me,
for all the things I've said,
about the bees and the birds
to ears that weren't hers,
and the places such phrases led.

I wonder if she'll forgive me,
for my failure to wait for her.
See the mate that she prayed for
has spent nights with strangers,
her patience I do not deserve.

I wonder if she'll forgive me,
for being chauffeured by such lustful hands
that drove around curves
that were neither mine nor hers,
knowing broad is the road to such ends.

I wonder if she'll forgive me,
for failing the faith we share,
like Cain I'm unAble,
to find her dad's favour,
spent more time preying than in prayer.

I wonder if she'll forgive me,
for the sins that stripped my clothes.
I undressed God's purpose
for pleasures that weren't worth the
exposure of my naked soul.

I wonder if she'll forgive me,
for intentions that were less than pure.
I'm now done chasing rhinestones
because out there is a diamond,
and my life belongs to *her*.

*—At some point in your life you're going to come face to face with
a woman you can't live without. And hopefully, if you're lucky,
your past won't be the reason you're forced to live without her.
Not everybody has a future that's willing to accept their past.
With that said...if your past was a resume' (which it probably
is)...would you get the job?*

Her V

-*Time is the maker, but timing is the trouble.*

i.

Yesterday I played like the boys
that her faith won't allow her to see.
Invisible was I, as she walked on by,
greeting everyone else but me.

ii.

Today I prayed like the man,
that I know she'll one day seek.
Asking God, if it's destined,
to send me directions
to wherever she, now, may be.

Her VI

—Just because you found it, doesn't mean it's yours...

I think I found her;
a goddess dressed like a sonnet
that I've neglected to read.

Each line defines perfection
so I'm guessing
she isn't for me;

or you.

Because like the sword in the stone,
there's none worthy to hold
the memory that her melody brings.

A reality, that
casually stings

over and over
again.

Nobody

They say you are nobody till somebody kills you.
And that—
has me confused.

Because as often as I was killed
I'm lying here still…
just a nobody
to somebody like you.

Sin

Her fingers spoke in parables.
Each touch narrating a sin I longed to commit.

Days slowly stripped into nights
as my Adam slipped inside
her Eve.

Her body was an Eden
I dare not leave–
Delilah;
my forbidden fruit.

And as I sipped water from her wine
she made arcs
that symbolized
the flood was near...

My fear thrusted into the safety of her
temple but my seed felt guilty
once safely inside.

Lying naked in
such sacredness
I could not hide…
from feelings of guilt
that refused to subside.

Once again,
we failed to abstain.
Using His name in varieties of vain,

over and over again.

Deep in her regret
was a tongue that spoke in tongues,
reciting scriptures to body parts
that weren't ours to own.

We fucked for forgiveness
And lied naked to atone,
sleeping in sin
before casting our stones.

Each morning we pray
for forgiveness alone,
despite sleeping in sin
and casting our stones.

Chicken Little

The sky is falling.

And I'm sure I would've caught her
if I wasn't busy falling
for you.

Simply Stars II

Let not our love be like the sun and the moon,
   fighting for existence
   only to exist in day for a night;
   breathing only for a time.

Nor like the clouds that predict the most
   unpredictable outcomes.

Instead,
let our love be like the stars;
always shining
despite immense darkness
and never retreating during the most heated moments.

Let our love be as high and as bright as the stars.

Let our love be as numerous and everlasting as the
   stars.

Let our love be simply stars,
                    simply amazing.

Long Distance I

Though miles apart never have I
seen a better couple than the stars and the sky.

Love fades by day, but dances by night.
Never in existence a more perfect sight.

Long Distance II

You're the sun
I'm the moon
Rarely we sleep
Together but forever
I promised you, *Me.*

And though I've been faithful
This distance is hard
You're surrounded by angels
And I'm falling for stars.

Ocean

Over the ocean, somewhere lost at sea,
my heart has set sail in search of *Me.*

And over the ocean, beyond the blue,
Me is lost at sea, in search of *You.*

Space

I asked her for space
but she never really knew,
that it was getting crowded
Cos I was making room for you.

London Bridge

The only bridge I dare not cross,
A toll of love, I've paid the cost.

Blessed be written, our history;
A bridge I've burned...continuously.

Epiphany

Wish I knew now
what I knew then;
such knowledge would save the world.

Because then I wouldn't have to
break these hearts just to
find another girl (like you).

Acrophobia

-There's a difference I think, between being afraid of heights...
And being afraid to fly.

I wish I saw the way she sees,
a sight to see her soar.

Such heights, I might,
despite the fright,
continue to endure.

April

You were his before you were mine;
another victim of poverty.

Poor timing has cost us a future
that I pay for every time you pass me by.

Magic

She laughed when I said,
"I believe in magic."

But I've seen things.

I've seen 'good morning' texts
Turn into a holiday
      "Hope all is well..."

I've seen
      "Sweet dreams, love..."
Morph into a Christmas
      "My fam says hi, I've been
      thinking 'bout you..."

And I'll be damned if that's not magic.

The way daily smiley faces
Become blue ticks
That suck consistency dry.

The way conversations disappear
With x's,
Last seen on May 26th;
It's December 1st...

And it hurts.

Hurts to watch Time saw a relationship in half
And yet,

She laughs,
When I say,
"Magic is real."

I've seen unstored numbers appear out of thin air with
        "I miss you"

I've seen 'Bae' become '912-401-7015',
And saw authors of 'I love yous'
Text "who's this?" in the blink of a July...

Which is why,
I say
magic is real.

Because only magic can turn 'forever'
into a forgotten memory.

Dear Flower I

Dear Flower,

Dance.

Like a butterfly on the heel of a Rose.

Rise above the feet that seek to stamp—
Heed your heart always.

For she is the keeper of your nine lives.

Live as if there's more.

Dear Flower II

Dear Flower,

Fly.

Like the fairies of a Dandelion stuck in a storm.

Reign over the weeds
that quenched their thirst
with your rainbow.

Whet their sharp tongues
with the flavour of *"no"*.

And know that your words
are a shovel.

And that seeds can be buried
alive.

Dear Flower III

Dear Flower,

Burn.

Like a Poinciana in summer
or like a Poinsettia in snow.

Show that your fire is constant
despite the change in their weather.

For whether warm hands hold
or lonely winds blow…

Your wick still hugs close its flame.

Dear Flower IV

Dear Flower,

Stand.

Like the daughter of a Sunflower seed.

You're a brown girl in a ring of Goliaths
that have no idea that the hearts they use as
stepping stones
can also be
    thrown.

Your aim is true.

Dear Flower V

Dear Flower,

Speak.

Like the tongue of a Tulip;
fluent in every colour of love.

Don't be silenced by the violence of wings
that never took you as high as promised.

Should you ever lose your way,
your hue is a map back to sanity
and your petals, breadcrumbs,
should you ever long for home.

Dear Flower VI

Dear Flower,

Love.

Like the lips of a Lily.

Know that your shape does not define your
    sovereignty of self.
For you are a deity.

Demand your worth.
Tax to touch your throne
and make them bend
to borrow your grace.

For yours is the kiss of life
or death…

Dare any to defy.

Dear Flower VII

Dear Flower,

Travel.

Wander like Dandelions in search of a pride,
but know that you are still a queen without.

Touch with thorns the tips that tore you from your
    twilight like deflowered Daisies
and blood them with the wrath of the Naked Lady
    they rage and rape to see.

Heal from the "love me nots" that ripped your reason
    without consent.

But please,
I beg you,
never change.

Dress as conservative as Chrysanthemums or as
    scandalous as an Apetalous angel.

For your body is yours and yours alone.
No matter how many times they try
to tell you differently.

-series inspired by:
"Dear Fat Girl"
- An excerpt from *Sans Roses* By Nikera Cartwright

Interlude -
For Those Who Cry Wolf II

Dear you,

Climb.
Climb that crystal stair.

Don't be discouraged by their courage.
Let them stare.

For few have seen a unicorn up close.

You're close,
So don't fall now.
You're almost there.

Just keep on climbing, honey.
You're almost there.

Part II: Coming To America

– A selection of immigrant related experiences
from a rather experienced immigrant.

Dipped

I packed up my life into two Sushi rolls and *dipped.*

—June.10.2017

Aisle One

It came from aisle one;
a two-legged three-year old
with more questions than I had answers for...

And in between her inquisition
she positioned herself
to
be
picked
up.

I...froze,
like a nigga in cop lights,
and breathed for what felt like the very last time
as she extended her two arms towards mine.

I...froze.

Looking from left to right for the *right*
Gender
Race
Or
Ethnicity...
but upon closer inspection
in every direction
it became clear
that it was just Claire
and me.

So I kneeled down,
master to slave,
wondering,
am I going to be punished for the skin color I chose to
wear today.

But not today.

Today she—
grabbed my hair
and stared,
asking,

  "Why is it so soft?"

She plays that way it seems.
Using all 5 senses to her advantage,
voiding the disadvantage I thought my melanin played.

And as I looked around
awaiting that sound that *"get on the ground"* made...
she
played.

We walked around for what seemed to be an eternity
as I searched for a reason to explain
why this child was clinging to me,
ever so close.

About a forever later came two pigs and an alligator
chasing the space in between my captor and me.

Again,

I froze.

Words were being spoken in a language that my
    anguish couldn't define
as I wondered if their thunder
was coming to her rescue
instead of mine.

My voice raced her words but lost
as she shouted,

   "Look, it's soft!"

to the judge and jury of what was sure to be–
an unfair trial.

But the little princess that dived
ignorance first into a stranger's arms
gave me a calm that superseded my greatness fear;

Being a black immigrant in her 'Merica.

Broke I

"You're broke,"
she said,
"not poor; there's a difference."

As if eviction notices spoke in nuance...

Creditors, to their credit,
pretend to understand
though late fees suggest that they don't.

I do, but I don't,
get it;
the unsolicited advice that suggests
that everything will be ok
from people that always are.

I guess birds could never understand
what it's like to walk for a living.

Broke II

Pity-filled coupons for nights on couches
expire with daily reminders that—
poverty is a reality.
And *broke* is just a Band-Aid concealing
a wound that will never heal.

Everything will *not* be ok.

People who suggest that there's a rainbow after every
    storm,
fail to realize that a rainbow doesn't last forever
and a storm lasts twice as long.

Meet The Parents I

She introduced me like a lepered stranger,
maintaining a distance consistent with shame.

Names soon forgotten shook heads before hands
as I,
palm exposed,
grasped at pocketed fists
that seemed all too eager
to swing.

Meet The Parents II

"He's my bi-polared angel," she smiled.
Joking that I give her heaven and hell simultaneously.

Shamelessly she–
dangles my secret amongst sharks,
fishing for laughs
knowing damn well that the colour of my skin
is like blood in holy water
and it's time
to prey.

I am almost certain that this is my last supper.

Meet The Parents III

She's biting the nails she once used to crucify me;
that's never a good sign.

Color-blind Christians *insisting*
I sleep on the couch
is a sin she can't forgive
from a saint she dare not cross;

her father;

holy in everything
except equality.

Meet The Parents IV

"I'm sorry" is a shorter sentence than "I told you so,"
but racial tension requires length...

So I told her,

"A colouring book is nothing
without its colour."

Meet The Parents V

I knew we reached the end
when she said that we began
as friends.

Meet the Parents VI

I walked away while she was still speaking
And she became heated.

Demanding that I, *respect* her,
thirty seconds after she spent the last hour
shouting–
>"The things you people call struggles
>are divisive..."

It's the first time she ever removed herself from the
dialogue.

The first time "our" became a "you."

You people.

"You people..." she said.
Right before demanding the respect she refused to give.

Meet The Parents VII

She said she understands now
and that she fears for me daily.

That I'm one traffic stop away from a misunderstanding
that would leave me standing six feet sideways.

She says this as if her new fears are the keys
to my forgiveness,
or a replacement for the words,

"Sorry. I was wrong."

But instead of an apology
she and her family annoyed me
by repeating,
unnecessarily,

"I won't apologize for being white."

It was then that I felt it necessary
to apologize for being black.

The American Dream

The *American Dream*
can be a nightmare
to anyone
that's *not*
American.

Black Panther

I waved at him.

Mr. 3ft. nothing,
dressed like something
out of a comic I once read.

"T'challa," I smirked.

He smiled.

Until April, May, or June
tuned in to our conversation.

"I'm sorry, what?"

"His costume, he's Black Panther..."

The kid looked away as April, or May,
ranted and raved for a ten-second eternity.

"How dare you?!"
She screamed.

"He's Batman!
You people really have some nerve."

There it was again.
That phrase.

You people...

The nerd in me quickly clashed with reality,
and suddenly,
I became
    'That man.'
the–
    "Black man…"

to a kid that saw nothing more than someone who
'got it.'

            "T'challa."
He whispered.
Looking at my feet because Summer clearly stole the
owers he had to look anywhere else.

An awkward silence was broken by Autumn's anger as
the panther,
my childhood hero,
was being dragged away like a wagon with a broken
wheel.

I guess M.J. had it all wrong,

It does matter,
if you're black or white.

Wildflowers I

Wild flowers grew where they lay,
haggard and helpless under a hopeless sky.

"There's space over there," he pointed,
"there's always space for the homeless."

Cali streets are kind that way,
breeding a unique sort of sympathy.

Begging is a price they can't afford
and a cost I'm not willing to pay;
pride will be the death of me,
I know.

But somehow…
I sleep better this way.

The first night is always the worst they say….
Well here's me hoping for the best.

Donald Numpt

Humpty Numpty sat on a wall
and never in all of my life,
have ever I hoped,
the words Mother Goose wrote
would one day, soon, be right.

45

I'll never forget the day
When a 45 brought the world to its knees
Threatening to fire
At sons of bitches
That refused to lift their—
Heads for a flag
That refused to fly
For them.

Land of The Fee

So here I am
In the Land of the Fees
Purchasing rights
With left fists raised
High enough to
Get their attention.

Which always comes at a price.

Here I am
Buying free speeches
With kneeled knees
That have me standing at
Heights synonymous with subjection,
Submission, and slavery.

Here I am
Shopping for liberties
With kind words and respect
Hoping that "yes sir"
Is the bullet proof vest the
Rest of America claims it to be.

Here I am
In a land
Where reparations are paid for,
Packaged and shipped
In the bottom of ships as
Programs and initiatives
That carry the phrases
"Get over it, it was a long time ago"

Here I am
Proud and free
And should I feel otherwise I'm free
To go back to wherever the fuck I came from
Because complaints cost extra
And suggestions for improvement will be taxed.

Here I am
At the cashier of a country
Where diversity is complimentary
But equality comes with an asterisk,
Feel free to buy into the opportunities
But you'd do well to note
That freedom is sold separately.

West Indian Ink

The lanky lecturer lectured a lesson that I will never
    forget.

He said,
sternly,
but ever so gently...

> "Be careful not to let the ink get on your skin,
> because once it gets on it'll never come off."

To everyone's surprise,
except mine,
a white-wine mixed with milk looking girl from the
    south of the class
pointed her paintbrush in jest...

> "I guess,"

she expressed,

> "Mecko didn't listen."

Offence

Unlike most of my friends,
I fail to take offence when ignorance
inquires about the state of my country.

Because in sharing that—

> *Iphones and Internet are present,*
> *but tree huts and loincloths aren't...*

I was able to peel the orange skin off
of yet another tangerine-shaped American who—

hides behind their rind
never finding the time to educate themselves
about things non-American.
A feat which seems to be translated as
un-American.

I stopped taking offence at statements that suggest that
I'm technically,
Jamaican.

Instead,
I reply,
sans arrogance,
with knowledge,
and trust that when my ignorance is exposed
they will do the same.

—You should never respond to ignorance
with arrogance.

An Observation

I've seen stares snatch souls from Hispanics that say
"*nigga*" frequently.

And seen teeth that meet street whenever Whites say it
equally.

It always amazes me how powerful that word has
become…to *them*.

It seems as if the word "*nigga*" offends Americans
more than any other nationality,

And, perhaps,
rightfully so.

Synonyms

I told her I was from *The Bahamas;*
"…technically Caribbean but definitely West Indian."

When she replied—
using the same tone that stone-cold stunners
anyone that has jack to say about
blacks
women
and
abortions—
        "You're still an African-American."

And despite my attempts to explain that,
I'm not even *American…,*
      she continued to spew her arrogant ignorance that
      was irrigated by a rooted hatred of white history.

Explaining how a—
"…*technically Caribbean but definitely West Indian man*"
couldn't be anything other than…
African.
American.

She stared again.
This time
with
utter
dis-
belief…

when I said Black and African American aren't
   synonymous.

She's still staring,
I think,
and I'm still smiling.

Pro-Black

She said that being Pro-Black
means to make sacrifices.

And that dating White, Latin, Asian or other
is none other
than an admission of self-hate;
a confession that I have no love
for anything
Black.

Well I'm sorry,
But my Mothers, Aunts, Sisters, and Friends don't
cease to exist just because
I didn't pick
you.

Coming to America I

Why is it hard for Americans to
understand that
the West Indies
isn't in Africa?

Prejudice

Today I saw a bumblebee
and that humble, honey suckling he—
or *she*,
sweet-lipped with wingtips
skinny-dipped into my
skyjuice.

Now just a short time later
after bumblebee said "alligator,"
my smile faded.

Anger rose as a fly dove—
feet first into my thirst-quenching cruise.
Sinking, without thinking,
my drink and its crew.

So naturally, of course,
in anger I tossed,
two "shoos" and a palm,
along with some obscene—

    "I mean,
    how dare he demean
    my drink!?"

Oh paid dearly, that he did,
with a sober-solid hit,
but I reckon,
it only took a few seconds
for Guilt to move on in.

Ever the squatter,
Guilt chastised the swatter,
for failing to see
the hypocrisy;

For a bumblebee I smiled,
just a passenger, passing by,
a soon to be murder scene.

Prejudice II

A butterfly landed on my cousin's shoulder;
he smiled.

I told him it was actually a moth;
he ran.

Well isn't that a subtle lesson in prejudice?

Prejudice III: Generalizations

A spider killed a butterfly,
When I was nine or ten,
I slashed the web,
And smashed his head
I've killed spiders ever since.

I climbed a tree to pick a fruit,
But stumbled on a bee,
It stung me twice,
Which wasn't nice,
So I swat each one I see.

Some ants bit my cousin once,
And they made her cry,
So every time I see an ant,
I make sure it dies.

–He was shot by a black guy and has hated me ever since. I'm
happy to report though, that after a few classes, he hates me a
little bit less.

Rain

I've never seen rain without clouds—
until today.

Clear blue skies
without a cloud to comfort
were conquered by
strange
drops
of
water
that
were
neither
wet
nor
wanted...
by me.

Strange, indeed.

But like everything else
in this life I lead,
I'm no longer
surprised.

—the day it rained in Sunny California.

The Fourth of July I

The sky is on fire again
but with a different sort of flame.

Hunter and hunted share hugs
under a burning hell
that both claim as heaven.

Disputes of who is devil
are designated for tomorrow
when sanity returns.

But on this day
red and white will knock on the door
of a pure black sky.

Pride will rise
towering prejudice in ways justice never could.

Today
fireworks are a heartbeat in a rather heartless world.

The Fourth of July II

I spent the *Fourth of July* around two different kids
at two different times.

One delighted in the fireworks;
the other in the gunshots.

Both curious of the aftermath.

The Fourth of July III

I spent ten minutes answering his question
and I'm still not quite sure if either of us understood
the answer to why
there isn't a black firecracker.

Moonlight

At night
we shine differently;
she an innocent yellow
and I
a guilty blue.

Fear I

My greatest fear is that they'll
shoot before I get a chance to
expl-

Fear II

My greatest fear is that she sees me as a threat
and not a tenant.

Resist

My car has two legs...
And so I drive
step by step
to places I could never call home;
this land is foreign to me.

Familiar are the faces I do not know,
speaking a language of violence
that silently grows...

Eyelids in white hoods are preserved in irony,
blaming my hoodie for what he considers a tiring
string of murders.

Descendants of herders that herd us as they heard us
    cry...
now hurt us with murders whether we resist or
    comply...

So *I*–
resist.

Shot

They like to tell you
what you could've done
to stay alive
as if getting shot
came with instructions.

Oppression

They're not oppressed…they're upset.

Angry that their "rights" are being shared amongst
those they have wronged.

They're angry.

Upset that equality has been expanded to include
colors, countries and choices that they once
condemned.

They're not oppressed…
but *protest* as if they were.

As if slavery stole their siblings in their sleep.
As if their wives were worn for pleasure.

They protest as if their land was stolen
or their blood spilled for personal gain.

They protest as if they were given new
names,
lives,
or lies to believe.

They protest as if *they* were the minority.

I wonder what they're fighting for?

Especially when they have it all.

Alt

Ghosts that toasted to slavery
now drink in freedom
on the wrong side of history.

So I wonder,
why are there so many, *so eager,* to join them?

Wildflowers II

I was told to uproot wildflowers that naturally grew
to plant roses that *didn't*.

I now understand how America was built;
a repeal and replacement of natural placements
with placeholders that hold an unnecessary grudge
    against immigrants.

I wish,
sans their ignorance,
that they could see,
we all came
from seeds.

Epilogue –
For Those Who Cry Wolf III

Dear you,

Don't go gentle into that good night
Rage against the machines that seek to
tell you differently
For you are more than just a wallflower

Your silence is the language of stars
So speak you beautiful galaxy!

I dare you, my dear you,

Speak!

For death is deaf to life
And you are a living constellation.

Remember
Life is what you make it
So don't get trapped in your own creation.

Part III: Civil War
— Sometimes we fight against ourselves.
Sometimes we win, sometimes we lose;
these are tales of war.

Based On
A True Story...

Describe Yourself in 60 characters or Less

Im a butterfly in search of a cocoon that I won't soon
outgr

Video Games

Being bi-polar is a rather interesting video game.

Imagine being Mario
and having to save Toad
by fighting Bowser.

Now imagine,
that in your head,
you're all three.

You're fighting yourself, to save your self, from yourself.

As Mario,
you try hard to be a hero,
but feel so fucking depressed
when you can't save the day.

As Toad,
you're the victim.
Helpless as always.
A short, 30-year old dependent that walks faster
than he runs.

As Bowser,
the world is against you.
You're the villain and you don't know why.
The love of your life comes willingly,
then after coming,
blames you for fucking her over,
instead of just fucking her.

She then leaves you for Mario;
the guy you were before;
the guy she never wanted;
the guy you *use* to be.

You're every character.
You play every role.
You're a fucking star.
Invincible until your time runs out.

And just like that,
We're out of time.

Video Games II

Fall in love with a hero
Someone who never gets tired of saving you

Someone who never runs out of lives

To be continued is their catch phrase
And they will continue till the end

You deserve a hero
Someone that will save you
From me.

Art Lessons I: Lines

A good drawing typically involves keeping the lines
you're comfortable with and erasing the ones you're
not.

But every so often you'll encounter a line that's just—
out of line.

It can't be erased and it doesn't fit in.
So you try to accommodate it as best you can,
either by drawing more uncomfortable lines, or
removing the comfortable lines around it that make it
seem out of place.

In some instances, you try to change the line itself,
because, after all, why should all the other lines suffer
because of this line's insubordinate nature?

In art, they'll tell you to fuck off.
Allow that line to live.
Some would even say, that line is the life of the party.

But in life, however,
that line is a problem;
that line is *the* problem.

And, unfortunately,
either it falls in line,
or it's erased.

By consensus or by choice.

I am that line.

Art Lessons II: Painting

I was taught that painting is simply putting the
right color in the right place.

I wish the same were true of *love*.

Art Lessons III: Colours

I love days like this;

Days when the paint drips in exactly the right direction
and has the audacity to dry in your favourite colour.

Explaining an Anxiety Attack
to a Non-Believer I

It's like the feeling you get when you run down an escalator but have to abruptly stop because someone is in front of you.

Explaining an Anxiety Attack
to a Non-Believer II

On a street corner near you, you'll find a traffic light. Located on that traffic light is a tiny little button that allegedly gives you permission to legally, and, I suppose, safely, cross the road.

You push this button, gently, and with a silly sort of trust, you wait your turn to cross.

After the first two minutes of waiting, you stop and wonder if you even pushed the button at all, because surely it shouldn't take this long for your request to survive the rubber death match to be processed.

So at this point, doubt creeps in and you begin to wonder if you should push the button again. Would a second push cancel the first? Would it reset the entire process? You're not sure. But such is the life you lead. And surety is a rarity. So you push it again, this time a little bit harder than the last.

You feel empowered. Ready to take on the world. As soon as the light changes, of course. So, once again, you wait.

Ever sure in your pushage, you continue to wait, but then another two minutes pass and the cars that seem to have stopped for your passage, have started to go again, yet the red hand of death remains unchanged. It glares at you. Almost challenging you to defy it, but you're patient. You always have been. And so, regardless of the dare, you wait. But waiting seems to be futile as yet another stoppage of cars come and go without a reward.

You begin to assess the situation. Did you miss the green signal? Is the button working? Are you stuck in a glitch? You ponder. And in pondering you notice the endless stream of cars stopping again.

The sign is still red, but it's a short distance and your legs are strong. You feel as if you can make it, if you walk, no, if you run fast enough. And so you do. And as the first toe touches the cross walk, the hand you've been obeying for the past 10 minutes finally changes to green. You don't have to run. You can walk. And so you do. But 2 seconds into your 20 yard walk across the deadly highway, the hand starts to count down and you realize, there's no way you'll make it across. And so you panic…it somehow went from 12 to 2 seconds and you're not even half way across yet. So you contemplate turning back, but you've come so far. Ten minutes too far.

Horns blow at you and middle fingers scream imprecations that are pregnant with anger, and as you look from left to right at your predicament....you break down.

You then remember your lessons about handling anxiety. You count to ten. In the fucking middle of the road, you are counting to ten. And then you try to assess the problem, because assessment, they say, is a key step to overcoming anxiety.

You begin to think. Was it the button? Or was it me? You notice some dude with shaved eyebrows shouting "dude" and you try to ignore him, but he's distracting. He causes you to lose your thoughts and so you try to count again. Wait, what number were you on? Oh right…"3, 4, 5…"

A lady, no wait, a running back, is coming at you ever so aggressively, and so you try to run away from her, but in your panic, you run towards her instead. You crash. Head first into her breast and mid disaster she holds you for a millisecond and whispers, "It's okay", while simultaneously returning middle fingers to the middle of the road.

You and your newfound hero walk…slowly at first, across the road you've crossed a million times before, and eventually, you make it to the other side. You try to thank her but she puts her fingers to her lips and disappears into a wonderful silence of understanding.

So now, it's just you again. You and a red hand that's staring at you in disgust. You're pissed. Annoyed. Distraught. More so at the button than yourself.

You call the button worthless. You feel deceived because the cartoons and movies you watched made you believe that little red buttons held all the fucking power in the world. "Don't press the red button..." they'd say. Well, you pressed it, and you can personally say that the television screen was wrong. That button had no power whatsoever. You then, as your nature, begin to overthink. That button left you powerless. It controlled you. And now, you're in awe. Television was right. That button causes nothing but trouble.

After catching your breath. You push the button again. Look left, then right, and run like a bat out of hell towards the chickens awaiting their turn die.

Identity Crisis I

I saw my reflection in a tea cup once;
unstable as ever.

Apple cinnamon eyes that faded with each sip
were a perfect representative of who I had become;

A half-empty cup with a misspelled name,
struggling to find my own identity.

Identity Crisis II

On Halloween,
I dressed up as myself
And scared no one else
But me.

– On being yourself

Sibling Rivalry I

She speaks less than I do
and I don't speak at all.

I guess we're *similar* in that regard.

But disregard the notion that we're
anything
alike.

Because like
day and night
she's fire
I'm ice
and upon collision
our decisions
just might—
clash.

But after the fallout
we're still quick to call out
each other's name.

She,
my sister,
ambitiously unchained

and I,
her brother,
no different,
the same.

Sibling Rivalry II - Crossing the Bridge

She's afraid of heights
and all my life
I swear I never never knew...

So I walked like a god
never sharing the thought
that I was quite scared too.

Oliver's Twist

He feared her more than he loved her, which, for a child Oliver's age, was commendable considering he even loved her at all. "That ole bitch" is what we called her, to her back of course, for in front of her face we had a different name; *Mom.*

Mom was an exclamatory sentence filled with imprecations and impropriety. Mom wore low-cut fades that added to her boyish appearance but stole from her feminine charm. She was smaller than the fights she picked, but what she lacked in size, she made up for in attitude. "A honeybee with the bite of a bear" is how my father described her; "Nope, just a bear" is how my sister's father would reply.

Perhaps she was a honeybee once, but by the time Oliver was born, the beers had taken their turn. "Good morning honeys" were replaced with "What the fuck do you want?" Tables that were once combed with breakfast now contained empty liquor bottles, half-finished word puzzles, and, of course, *Oliver.* We knew better than to be at home when Mom woke, but Oliver didn't. We found refuge at summer school, but Oliver didn't. Instead, he clung close to the hands that hit him more than they held him; hands that tore through our faces like an oar through water.

I can still recall Mom's reaction when Oliver first said– "I love you." Like a deer caught in headlights, she stood briefly before shrugging sorrowfully and shimmying away.

We stood in shock, not at her response but at Oliver's admission. He...loved her? Perhaps the innocence of his youth sheltered him from the reality we'd long accepted, but his willful ignorance had surely betrayed him for the word "love" was fictional in our household. Love shared its non-existence with Santa Claus, the Tooth Fairy and Fathers. She had personally ensured us that such things were pure folly and we all believed her; except Oliver.

Poor Oliver. A victim of recidivism, he danced again with the danger of enlightenment as he shouted for the second time in his 10-year existence, "I love you," only to be greeted with an awkward silence and a Gorgon glare. Even echoes knew better than to repeat such phrases, but sadly, Oliver didn't.

"I love you mom," he sanguinely shouted to her back, and then to the door that acquiescently opened, then closed, as she quickly departed.

For a minute, I blanked out; kidnapped by a nostalgic moment. I remembered saying, *no,* writing, those words once. *I Love you.* Carefully crafted in my newfound cursive penmanship on a birthday card that she now used as a cup coaster.

Perhaps, like his eldest sibling before him, Oliver, too, was caught up in the moment. It was, indeed, Mother's Day, so I chalked it up as an easy mistake, until, a few weeks later, Oliver persisted. Dressed in ignorance and glowing with naiveté he reiterated,

"I love you, mom."

She was no longer a deer in headlights. She was now Bambi's mother, shot unsuspectingly. She showed weakness, emotion, and could it be, for a second, compassion? Whatever it was lasted all but for a second before she began laughing hysterically like an asthmatic hyena, shortly gasping for air, only to reply with, "*You better!*" as she galloped away.

That was the last we ever saw her...as a mother.

Like smoke with no escape, tears welled in Oliver's eyes, but I was determined not to let them fall. I punched him as hard as I could, for it would be because of the pain I inflicted that he ever sheds a tear; because of me and not because of *her*.

Love was a foreign language to her, foreign in a way of which it was seemingly communicated, but never fully understood. Simply put, we weren't aborted, we never starved, and we were educated, privately; tuitions always paid in full. As much as I hated her, I forced the others to be grateful. For what she lacked in kindness, she made up for in wealth. There were always toys, candy, and video games to keep us distracted; distracted from what she wasn't; from what she never tried to be; a mother.

As the eldest, I made it a priority to read my siblings stories of Orphan Annie and little Oliver Twist, changing the names of course, trying to convince them, and myself for that matter, that though there is a difference between being cared for and being loved, it is far better to be cared for, but mistreated, than loved, but homeless. We may have never been loved, but we were, certainly, never homeless.

Like smoke with no escape, tears welled in my eyes as they lowered her 6 feet higher than where she, quite possibly, truly belonged. But before my eyes gave birth to even a single tear, a hand tore through my face like an oar through water. It was Oliver's. The mourners stood in shock, like deer in headlights; some afraid, and some confused. But amongst the confusion, there stood a few siblings, laughing like asthmatic hyenas because they truly understood. Smiling painfully, but grateful for the return of such a fateful favor, I got up and stared silently at each and every one of them. A few seconds before the silence was broken by a wayward wail, I communicated, non-verbally, in a way that only siblings can, something that I'm sure they fully understood. In response, like a trained choir, in complete synchronicity, they all replied, *"You better!"*

Sincere smiles swam across empty pools as we all, unashamedly, walked away before the first shovel ever touched the ground.

Lightskinned: A Tale of Two Crayons

I broke his Black crayon
Just the other day

Then snapped the Brown
Such an awful sound
These lessons tend to make

He cried, he cried
Or so it seemed
For his tears were quite short lived
Because right to his left
Were the Pinks and the Reds
The *"pretty ones"* or so they say...

Melanin

I gotta remind her everyday day that—
there's no such thing as *'too black'*.

And I gotta remind him everyday that—
there's no such thing as *'not black enough'*.

Icarus

He's best friends with the sun.
Together they'd play tag with timezones
and double date clouds that cried for attention.

I suppose that's how I was made;
a pot of gold at the end of a rainbow he once flew
    through.
Son of an eagle, yet the ground is all I ever knew...

I wonder if my father ever knew
that both sons
had different views
of *him.*

Icarus II

Pilots never know their passengers
and maybe that's all I ever was;

unclaimed baggage
seated in the carriage
of a bird with iron claws.

Tuesdays With Rain

We meet around the corner every Tuesday and rain. Tears fall from the sky as we exchange pleasantries; some Tuesdays more pleasant than others.

"Morning Mildred."

"You cocksucker you! You gon' pay me
my money! You hear me Perry, you gon-"

"It's me Millie, remember? Jackson?"

"Jack be nimble, Jack be quick, Jack jumped over the candle stick. That *you* Jack?"

"Yes, Millie, it's–it's me."

"Well whatcha standing in the rain for?
'Monia ain't a woman to mess with.
Come on in."

This Tuesday was pleasant.

'In' was the outside porch of an old, wooden hut, crooked in its posture but yet stubborn in its stance. The same could be said of Millie.

Millie was…interesting. To strangers she was a vile vagrant that verbalized violence towards anyone in her vicinity, but to me, however, Millie was a history book; an encyclopedia of historical knowledge with just a few pages missing or out of order. Millie had often described to me–and anyone patient enough to listen–in detail, decade-long plots that were now being followed through. She spun tales of political corruption and betrayal that simple visits to any local government office–or prison cell depending on which perspective you valued–could easily confirm. Few things blurted in her manic states were found to be false and even then a stench of truth clung close. How she obtained these stories were often a mystery to anyone who took her seriously, though only a few people, including myself, ever did.

About two decades ago, during a close electoral race between two political parties, Millie became the subject of a curious rumor. It was rumored that Millie was an undocumented immigrant turned mistress to a prominent politician, whom, upon further inquiry, flatly denied such allegations. The allegations were so absurd that almost nobody outside of the conspirators believed them, however, doing my due diligence as a nosy citizen, I felt compelled to inquire directly from the source.

What was supposed to be a thorough interview filled with intense cross-examinations turned into a budding friendship. Millie was quite the entertainer. Some weeks Millie played characters from her favorite 80's sitcoms, while other weeks she channeled famous entertainers. The days she believed herself to be Etta James were my favorite.

"At Last…" she would sometimes sing.

As crazy as Millie was, she definitely could carry a tune. Sometimes weeks of characters and famous celebrities would go by before I ever came into contact with the real Mildred; a wise lady that a great injustice had fell hard upon. I was warned to take her stories with a grain of salt, but for some reason, I loved the taste.

One had to be careful of which "Mildred" they approached. Depending on the day you visited, you might get saliva instead of sensible conversation, the latter of which, by the standards of the sane, wasn't exactly sensible at all, but I stuck around for every word, regardless of the sentence they came with. Sometimes I would broach the subject of the infamous rumor with Millie, being careful to sound as little like her hecklers as possible, only to receive bits and pieces of memories long forgotten. Whether or not she was an undocumented immigrant was still a mystery to me, but one thing was certain...she was definitely a politician's mistress. She knew too many random details and inner secrets of a house I once called home for me to believe anything different. She spoke of objects long lost, then found, in termite-infested attics and painted accurate pictures of every scratch and stain in parts of a house that was off-limits to me for years.

Obtaining information from Millie was quite the task, but my patience and resilience against imprecations and stony objects often paid generously.

My father wasn't one for rumors. The day after he heard of the accusations and rumours surrounding Mildred he sought hard for her demise. Through bribed police efforts and pressured social workers, his campaign to remove Millie from the ruined castle she claimed began to increase greatly leading up to the end of his political reign. His attempts of having her arrested for slander or inducted into medical institutions for health concerns failed miserably, however, and eventually, he seemed to disregard her entirely. It wasn't until he got word that I would meet with her frequently that his efforts reignited. His latest attempt involved inciting trespassing charges only to see Millie's release secured by an unknown relative with possession of documents that, to the shock of many, myself included, verified Millie as the owner of the dilapidated dungeon. And just like that, within a few days of her release, Millie was back on her throne, running from and or attacking anyone that would see her moved.

His increased efforts jogged my suspicions, but I could never bring myself to confront him directly, for we were never as close as the title of father and son would suggest. If it weren't for my grandfather taking me to visit my father's office every weekend, I suspect I would've never seen him; sometimes I wish I never did.

Some Tuesdays were more pleasant than others. Though cloudy in her shine, the rain never touched the ground. So instead of walking around the corner to Millie's, I decided to walk past instead. I strolled by slowly, only to find, in my amusement, a few Jehovah's Witness' representatives running away from Millie's missiles. "She always had wonderful aim," I thought to myself. As one of the ladies scurried past me, I smiled at her, invitingly, and offered up some quick advice.

"She won't talk to you unless it's raining."

The lady smiled embarrassingly in return.

"Oh, do you know her?"

"Yeah," I sighed shamefully, but added, rather confidently,

"She's my mom."

The Boy Who Cried Wolf I
—Ideation

Sometimes I sit and watch the mangoes fall to their
   death.

One by one
as they surf the distance between heaven and hell,

I wonder...

Has anyone ever told them
that they have so much to live for?

The Boy Who Cried Wolf II
—Pep-talk

The street lights are too bright for private conversation,
so I whisper to myself
and hope to God that I'm listening
when it's all said and done.

The Boy Who Cried Wolf III
–Prevention

I was told to seek help before it's too late;
well I'm early.

Fighting through tears
that smear a carefully written number
on a carelessly torn paper;
my savior,
is only one more number away...

It rings; *twice.*

The chill in my bones heats up
as the frog that was once stuck in my throat
croaks for what may be the very last time.

And as I'm–
about to–
share 30 years of
"why am I still here"
to Jesus,
Buddha,
or whoever the hell would have
picked
up
the
phone…

I groaned.

Defeated in whatever victory I thought I had gained
by just seeking help again and again...

I groaned.

Because the person on the other line
wasn't human like you and I
but, instead,
just a carefully automated tone
that was 2 minutes too long.

And if my tears could've cried
I'm sure they would've tried
when my automated angel said

"please try again later."

Ironic, I suppose,
because I most certainly did.

The Boy Who Cried Wolf IV
–Free Falling

I visited the streets in my favorite songs
Hoping to live a little while longer.

But chords are shorter than curves
Ending seconds before my second attempt...

The Boy Who Cried Wolf V
–Anxiety

I can still recall that time when
my mind held my lungs hostage.

Every breath in wanted out at a pace
my thoughts couldn't keep up with.

It was then that
I concluded,
I'm dying;

I hope.

The Boy Who Cried Wolf VI
-Fast Car

L.A. nights are half-written memories;
love letters sloppily scribbled on street signs
in a language I used to speak…
addressed to a person I used to be.

Brake lights merge like blood veins in the distance
and in this instance
I'm a message in a broken bottle;

an unfinished obituary edited by stoplights
that play tag with a will that's unwilling to live…
in search of a funeral from freeways that are unwilling
    to give—
        the exit I desperately seek.

Speed limits wave goodbye
as I—
drive like a plagiarized signature
into my final breath,
hoping for an officer to save me from a death
that's sure to come.

The Boy Who Cried Wolf VII
-Confessions

I told her I was suicidal
and she called me a coward.

Slapping me with scriptures
that I've long ago evicted.

I went to war with demons that had more reasons
   than her,
as to why I should live a little while longer.

See, in my mind,
life has a word count
and I fear I've reached my limit.

On Mental Health

My body is like Ash's Charizard…
strong
but
stubborn.

Actors

I was taught that love is 'patient' and 'kind'
An interesting theory I suppose

But when placed into practice
It seems we're all just actors
envying each other's role.

Hurricanes I: The Rooftop

Momma bought oil for the door
before she bought wood (for the window)…
Anoint the house
but neglect the car that's ready to go?

Slow shook her head
"No faith, no glory"
she stubbornly said.

Would if I could…

Be just a bit older
put her on my shoulder
just to show her that—
together…
we're still shorter than
the height of the flooding water she keeps blessing.

But lessons are sometimes stubborn teachers
as I reach for
her outstretched hand
that fate now demands
I let go.

–Hurricane Survival 101

Hurricanes II: Neighbor to Neighbor

Can't leave the—
first key I ever turned

Learned— *right there*
how to pick pear and
skin fish, this—
this here for the kids after I'm gone
so I gotta hold on.

But don' let me stop you dear
You can fear the fair weather warnings
but come morning I gon' be right here
helping these man made doors fight against
these God given winds.

"And if God wins..." you say?

Well...honey
let's just hope my sins can swim.

- Hurricane Survival 101

Hurricanes III: Holding On

How they gon let—
water from heaven scare 'em
Bin' here since I was seven
and neva since 53'
has a lil bit ah rain scare lil ole me...

You'll see
come morn
I'll be right here
holding on.

- Hurricane Survival 101

Hurricanes IV: Mister, Mister

The Mister down the way
who showed us his gun whenever we'd play—
too close to his mango tree,
now needs help; he has to leave.

Those stubborn roots
that threatened to shoot
when fruit were picked,
now needs to be picked up.

And it's just his luck...
that on that day he shot,
when our sheep cried wolves
because some shepherds haven't forgot.

And it's just his luck...
that on that day he shot,
saving the frightened fruits that he once wished would
rot.

Hurricanes V: The Adjustment Bureau

To the left of what's left
stands a righteous wrongdoer who—
with the stoke of his pencil,
proceeds to pen down—
in an uppity sort of way—
exactly what he thinks I'm worth.

And if I let him tell it,
my thirteen and seven years
of blood sweat and tears are worth no more than
the doorbell that no longer rings…

It took him twenty minutes to tell me
what twenty years of my life was worth
and—
it hurts…

It hurts to know that
his short-hand
double-spaced sentences
will be the judge that sentences
me to life
on the streets
sans the storm.

- Hurricane Survival 101

Hurricanes VI : Waiting

This ain't nothing like
back in my day;
winds strong 'nuff to blow Satan 'way.

See you young people don't know bout prayer,
go'on baby,
I'll be right here,

waiting.

- Hurricane Survival 101

The Little Mermaid

The sorrow of tomorrow
will stick like the sand.

Arms will follow hands to backs that—
some say,
should've never been turned.

As if a wave can't escape a gaze…

Sympathy will sink at the shores of the sure.
The– *"Sure wouldn't have been my child!"*
will surely have their say.
As they pull their kids closer than getting older would
ever pull them away.

Death…surely has a way
of making fools of man.
But how dare he
come near *she*;
a little girl who built her house upon the sand.
Castles amongst assholes who wouldn't understand
that—
a blink
or a yawn
is all it takes
for that coward Death to make yet
another escape
with beauty.

His "too soon touch" will truly
start a war of words back home…
as borrowed sympathy burrows skin deep
when casting their stones;
as if they are without sin.

As if they in their play
never missed the moment that—
caused their child's grin
to fade into tears.

Her death is a lesson learned some would carelessly say
as if that lesson lessens what would be felt today.

I just wish that—
somehow, some way,
that seven-year-old had eight more lives to play.

I just wish that—
somehow, some way,
that seven-year-old had eight more lives to play.

–For Elnora Bullard
R.I.P.

Before and After

Why do the greatest acts of humanity
happen *after* tragedies
instead of *before* them?

Hugs

Our hugs are lessons in humanity.

Conversations

I'm a lifetime member of
conversations that end
in disappointment.

Al Simers Jr.

I watch them.

All head nods and smiles as he tries to remember their
    names.

In between their patience and pity
he steals rich glances at people he has told he loves
though he cannot remember when or why.

His eyes fly from one face to another
in hopes to discover—
some familiar
friend
or *foe.*

Because Lord knows there's no hell
like lying in bed
awaiting your turn
to die.

Life

Sometimes I question life.

What's the sense of being the author
if you can't write your own ending?

Him

"Listen to them. Children of the night. What music they make."
—Dracula

A slave to the silence
he watches them dance
as they tango like mangoes
drunk on a branch...

They're not smooth
but it's not their moves that matter
it's the message

Written by a system
too cursed to bless them...
with a penny
or a kind word.

Their voices fall on deaf ears
because, like its maker,
Gravity hasn't been kind

And since the pockets of the plenty
rarely share a penny
it's no wonder they can only afford a small,
piece of mind.

Time watches as their hands chase second and third
     injections
to stimulate mental erections

See the streets were their only protection
as they were fucked by a reality
that just...came too fast.

Their cries for help are passed around
like unwanted hand me downs
Swimming in a religion called Hope
most have already drowned;

Poor souls,
baptized in potholes...
worshipping red lights
to them Heaven is a paved road.

Their bathroom has no doors,
because financially they're piss poor
You'll need more than a penny to begin
to think of how much shit they hold in.

I know He sees them.

But yet...He just watches them dance,
as they tango like mangoes
till they fall from the branch.

I know He listens,
He love's their melody;
Poverty pulls the strings
and Death holds the keys.

I know He listens,
He love's their melody;
Poverty works the strings,
and Death plays the keys.

Hallucinations

Sometimes,
I see things.

Hallucinations hibernating in memories
I never made.

Depression

I googled depression just to see what I look like...

And if what I saw was true,
I guess I'd constantly ask
if I were okay, too.

Almost Christian

Sometimes I regress
and lie naked with the patrons of everything I reject.

I find it hard to sleep knowing that I have slept
in places with faces I seem to forget.

I'm a hypocrite in every aspect of *The Word*.

Time Flew by

i.

Time flew by on rainy days,
Where hurricane winds kissed lonely waves
Still a stranger to life, with death I played,
As time flew by.

Time flew by on a summer breeze,
Where tire swings danced with tamarind trees,
Beyond the beach, I saw birds make bees,
As time flew by.

Time flew by on musical chairs,
Where love came dressed as truth or dare,
I pushed her down, did she know I cared?
As time flew by.

Time flew by on high-school games,
Where love notes flew on paper planes,
"No" meant *"maybe"*, damn, what was her name?
As time flew by.

Time flew by on life it seems,
Where broken hearts met guitar strings,
Life was almost cut short in vein,
As time flew by.

Time Flew By

ii.
I feel like a tourist
since time has flown by
Visiting tomorrow
in someone else's life
A slave to the present,
working for today,
punished for escaping
to yesterday
Where marbles roll
and Pluto exists
Where the dead could be brought back
with a dragon ball wish
It's hard to believe, but since time flew away,
I've grown old, but not up, still a kid at play.

Success

One day I hope to be successful.

Failure is far too often an option
when trying to end it all.

Failure

I've failed many times it seems,
A feat I'm quite proud of.

Because as much as I've tried
I'm still here despite
trying to end it all.

Selfish

Selfish is the word most commonly used
when refusing my reasoning that it's my right to
choose
    death.

Legos

Here's a
lego-like love
bubble-wrapped and packaged for the–
next daydreamer that's failed to see the–
nightmares behind
turning water into wine,
especially when I'm–
that glass that's so easily broken.

Devil's Pie

Savages ravaged an already rationed heart,
but far be it from me
to not save you a piece
of the Devil's pie.

Theism

There are some non-believers that deserve *heaven*.

There are more believers that deserve
hell.

Nightmares

Sometimes I read my nightmares bedtime stories.

Nightmares II

It often disturbs me when I realize that a nightmare is also a *dream*.

Pity Parties

Pity parties aren't fun when other people crash them.

Spectrum

Sometimes I wonder what he's thinking
behind that smile that never fades

We all agree,
he's *special,*
but I assure you,
I define 'special' differently.

Inaudible

Being heard is one of the hardest things to do
When in the company of people who have so much to say

(Bi)Polar Opposites I
- Civil War: Me Myself and Mornings

The Sun is smiling again;
his yellow stained grin hidden by Eyelids that swim
nakedly with a darkness
that refuses to drown.

"Stop crying..." their southern neighbors would say
as they drank each tear away,

"She's back."

Nosy Ears that were once heir to symphonies,
relay the message with sympathy...

"She's back."

At the preaching of these words,
the congregation can be heard;
Shoulders shuddering
And Lungs stuttering,
preparing for judgments they don't deserve...

Fear fornicates with my Fingers and as my Voice labors
    and lingers...
I whisper wasted words to *Her*...

"Not today. Not today." I say...
As if my voice could keep her away...

She's back.

(Bi)Polar Opposites II
- The Great Depression

The furtive *Morning* that spent the night in someone
else's sight slowly strolls in on orange high heels with
the breath of another room. She never knocks before she
enters; eager to meet the darkness I now call home.

She seduces the sheets that help my sins sleep,
awakening the demons that my friends have yet to meet;
there's no doubt about it...*She's back.*

She's back with this choir of friends that have acquired
this trend of hugging me.
They misdiagnose my affliction and fulfill it with
prescriptions that involve loving me
as I rage, rage, against the rising light.

"Are you even trying?" they would ask,
As I pray that they, too, shall pass.
And as day two, near its end,
I pray for the comfort of my darker friends;
the silence of Midnight,
and the eyes of Moon,
Morning may be back,
But Day promised me she'll be gone soon;
I hope.

Because the *Morning* that breathes life into this
depression that every sunrise has given me,
has no idea that she's killing me;
                                    softly.

(Bi)Polar Opposites III
-The Morning After Pill

Morning has broken

Fresh from the world she forces herself on me

And in my weakness we found completeness
as she clothed and undressed me...
over and over again.

I'm tortured inside,
but to the public eye I pretend...
As if sleeping with my enemy
will give birth to friends.
Well, perhaps...
it did.

Because hidden in my smile
they sense how I really feel;
pity for the parties that my presence tends to kill
as they assure me—

"Everything will be okay."
It won't .

Intoxicated by their inquiries,
I stumble away

Returning to sender, those annoying letters like
R, U, O, K...

Because *I'm not.*

But I smile a lie, as I depart,
like the dove from the ark
Hoping they would never see
that the flood isn't over for me…

My eyes continue to walk on water.
despite my faith being strong.

And as my tear ducts continue to dream of one day
becoming swans…
I maintain my composure.

And as my cups runneth over,
they are sipped by two soldiers who continue to
repeat,

"Not today."

"Not today," they would say,

as they drank each tear away…

(Bi)Polar Opposites IV
-The *Calm* after the *Storm*

A lonely breeze flirts with the tease that is my Sunset;
my reason to go gentle into this good night.

Stars are the angels that carry me
six feet from where each *Morning* has buried me;
oh, how grateful am I?

Grateful for the shadows that comfort my fear,
assuring me that in my loneliness,
there's always someone there...
to *guide me.*

Evenings are my Eden;
my Eve sent to hide me
from those who continue to scout,
for reasons why every season the mockingbird
    never wants out.

But lately, it's crazy,
how I just stare at the gems in the sky that slowly
    appear...
wishing they would stay,
reliving the living moment when I chose to live life
one day...at a time.

Fixed upon a star,
I slowly compare
this life sans the sun;
my heaven is near.

INDEX - Part I: Her

INDEX - Part II: Coming To America

INDEX - Part III: Civil War